My First Acrostic
All About Me

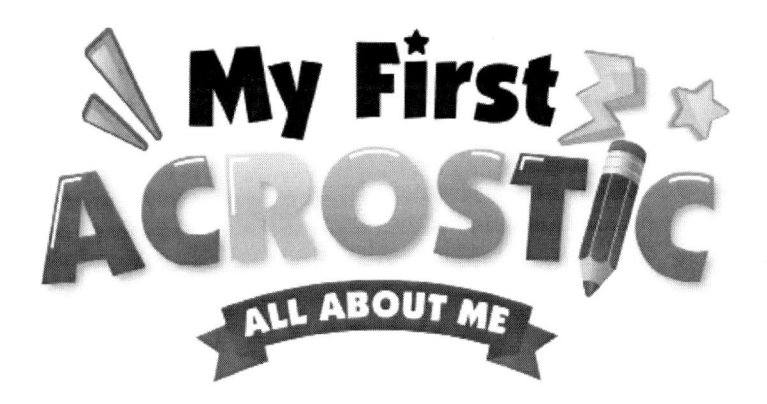

Amazing Verse

Edited By Kelly Reeves

First published in Great Britain in 2020 by:

Young Writers
Remus House
Coltsfoot Drive
Peterborough
PE2 9BF
Telephone: 01733 890066
Website: www.youngwriters.co.uk

All Rights Reserved
Book Design by Ashley Janson
© Copyright Contributors 2019
Softback ISBN 978-1-83928-695-7

Printed and bound in the UK by BookPrintingUK
Website: www.bookprintinguk.com
YB0429F

Dear Reader,

Dear Reader,

Welcome to a fun-filled book of acrostic poems!

Here at Young Writers, we are delighted to introduce our new poetry competition for KS1 pupils, *My First Acrostic: All About Me*. Acrostic poems are an enjoyable way to introduce pupils to the world of poetry and allow the young writer to open their imagination to a range of topics of their choice. The colourful and engaging entry forms allowed even the youngest (or most reluctant) of pupils to create a poem using the acrostic technique, and with that, encouraged them to include other literary techniques such as similes and description. Here at Young Writers we are passionate about introducing the love and art of creative writing to the next generation and we love being a part of their journey.

From pets to family, from hobbies to idols, these pupils have shaped and crafted their ideas brilliantly, showcasing their budding creativity. So, we invite you to proceed through these pages and take a glimpse into these blossoming young writers' minds. We hope you will relish these poems as much as we have.

Contents

Buildwas Academy, Buildwas

Amelia Nock (7)	1
Evelyn Macdonald (6)	2
William Roy Plimmer (6)	3
Grace Downing (6)	4
Sydney Ann Biddulph (5)	5
Zachary Evans (5)	6
Keira Leigh Paget-Jarrett (5)	7

Cheadle Hulme Primary School, Cheadle

Rocco Pearson (5)	8
Ayaan Majid (5)	9
Jessica Healen (5)	10
Charlotte Grace Marsden (6)	11
Ellen Travis (6)	12
Libby Manion (5)	13
Zidane Yahya Naveed (6)	14
Raya Malik (5)	15
Jessica Rose Payne (5)	16
Mila-Rose Usher (5)	17
Isaac Paul (5)	18
Noah Waite (5)	19
Ellie Marsden (5)	20
Theo Davison (5)	21
Ella Boyd (6)	22
Olivia Heritage (5)	23
Beatrice Blake (6)	24
Hugo Tatton (5)	25
Imaan Maya Sheikh (5)	26
Imogen Walker (5)	27
Aariya Knight (5)	28
Sebastian O'Neill (5)	29
James Bailey (5)	30
Charlie Francis Coombes (5)	31
Elsa Harling Kington (5)	32
Georgia Andrew (5)	33
Saul David White (5)	34
Camilla Eaton (5)	35
Henry Charles Fitzmaurice (5)	36

Fig Tree Primary School, Hyson Green

Asiya Husna Sageer (6)	37
Abbas Saqib (6)	38
Yahya Salahudeen Khan (6)	39
Abdussami Butt (7)	40
Zaynab Chishti (6)	41

Gilbert Heathcote Nursery & Infant School, Whittington Moor

Freddie Jack G (5)	42
Kali-Rose B (5)	43
Phoebe Launt (5)	44
Autumn Belle Barnett (6)	45
Suhrit Gudekota (6)	46
Malayah Jayne D W (6)	47
Courtney S (5)	48
Sophie R (5)	49
Callen Alec W (5)	50
Holly W (5)	51
Ellis R (5)	52
Sienna Mae Guyles (5)	53
Khadija S (5)	54
Millie Grace Houghton (6)	55
Ffion Elizabeth L (6)	56
Keira Elouise K (5)	57
Eden P (5)	58

Cory Max Shaw (5)	59
Lilly hodgkiss (5)	60
Demi Amber Taylor (5)	61
Kairi Kiers D W (5)	62
William Toft (6)	63
Faith C (5)	64

Hannah Ball School, High Wycombe

Muhammad-Zayed Zaman (6)	65
Finley James Brittain (6)	66
Aleema Afzal (6)	67
Lily Miranda Rigby (7)	68
Annetta Williams (6)	69
Owais Akhtar (6)	70
Mia Grace Green (7)	71
Ayaan Abbas (6)	72
Kira Zielinska (6)	73
Freddie Bailey Stevens (6)	74
Nicholas Paraskiv (6)	75
Antony Kupiec (6)	76
Brooke Ives (5)	77

Lady Alice Primary School, Greenock

Caleb Hamilton (7)	78
Morgan Vicki Crossan (6)	79
Alan Docherty (7)	80
Orla McMillan (6)	81
Aleksandra Da Fonseca (6)	82
Summer Williams Docherty (6)	83
Zak Arthur (7)	84
Deryn Paul (6)	85
Kian Deehan-Cowan (7)	86

Normanhurst School, North Chingford

Noah-Hussain Mahmood-Gupta (5)	87
Toyosi Francesca Fagbemiro (6)	88
Kehanique Lowe (6)	89

Francesco Chechile (7)	90
Eden Ryan (6)	91
Alicia Shakeel (6)	92
Lillie Durrant (6)	93
Erin Fernandes (6)	94
Farah Escoffery (6)	95
Zakariya Kodabuckus (5)	96
Korai Masters (6)	97
Emily Freedlander (5)	98
James Rapacki-Gladwell (5)	99
Kelly Ana Tranchand (5)	100
Irina Khairutdinova (5)	101
Nina Evans (6)	102
Izah Mirza (5)	103
Emran Qazi-Hoq (5)	104
Enis Hacimusa (6)	105
Caitlin McGuinness (6)	106

Roughwood Primary School, Rotherham

Ruby Hannaford (6)	107
Layla Rose Evans (6)	108
Holly Garrity (6)	109

St Peter's Primary School, Paisley

Sophia Taylor (7)	110
Joe Hannigan (8)	111
Orla Hannigan (8)	112
Joanna Shibu (8)	113
Aiden Mark McCafferty (7)	114
Leah Jackson (7)	115
Brandon Allison (7)	116
Mialena Craig (8)	117
Andrew Herd (8)	118
Ethan Kennedy (8)	119
Ciaran McCall (8)	120
Ellie Fadian (8)	121
Niamh Banaghan (7)	122
Max William Crawford (8)	123

St Thomas Of Canterbury Catholic Primary School, Coalpool

Olivia Highway (6)	124
Donald Munachimso Nwonyi (7)	125
Saoirse Beau Larmour (6)	126
Nelly Baumgardt (5)	127
Hanna Skulska (6)	128
Orla Rae Larmour (5)	129
Benjamin Tryjankowski (6)	130
Oliwier Donaj (6)	131
Skyla Kenfack (6)	132

The Poems

All About Amelia

A melia is my name
M ummy and Daddy hug me
E verybody in my family loves me
L ovely flowers are my favourite thing to smell
I ce cream is my favourite snack
A nimals, my favourite is a cheetah.

N aughtily knocking on doors is my favourite thing to knock on
O scar, my cat, doesn't like me
C ooking with my grandma makes me and her happy
K ingly cake is my second favourite snack.

Amelia Nock (7)
Buildwas Academy, Buildwas

All About Evelyn

E lephants are my favourite animals
V ery exciting Harry Potter sticker book is what I like to do
E ating crunchy peanuts is my favourite snack
L ovely flowers I like to smell
Y ellow used to be my favourite colour
N ice friends I have to play with.

Evelyn Macdonald (6)
Buildwas Academy, Buildwas

All About William

W riting stories is my favourite thing at school
I like eating chocolate
L ovely big brother
L ittle lions are so cute
I love dinosaurs
A nts are scary
M um and Dad love me.

William Roy Plimmer (6)
Buildwas Academy, Buildwas

Grace's Poem

G oats are my favourite animal
R unning because I like exercise
A pples are my favourite because they're crunchy
C ake is my favourite
E lephants are not my favourite.

Grace Downing (6)
Buildwas Academy, Buildwas

Sydney's Poem

S wimming is my favourite
Y oghurt is my favourite
D ancing is my favourite
N ice person
E lephants are my favourite animals
Y oghurt is yummy.

Sydney Ann Biddulph (5)
Buildwas Academy, Buildwas

Zach's Big Book Of Poems

Z achary likes playing small and shiny Lego.
A pples are my favourite fruit.
C omputers are what I like.
H appy people, I like them.

Zachary Evans (5)
Buildwas Academy, Buildwas

All About Keira

K angaroos are my favourite
E lephants have big feet
I guanas run so fast
R abbits eat carrots
A ll animals I love!

Keira Leigh Paget-Jarrett (5)
Buildwas Academy, Buildwas

Play

P enguin and Lizard are playing in the soil
L izard said, "Look at all those baboons playing in the streets there."
A t a very muddy bit, they jumped in muddy puddles and played diggers too
Y ou are very muddy, you need a bath to wash off all the mud and you can play in it too.

Rocco Pearson (5)
Cheadle Hulme Primary School, Cheadle

Play

P eople like to play on a sunny day
L ook around you, people are playing, Libby Lizard is playing
A lexsanda likes to play, everyone likes to play
Y ay, let's play everyone!

Ayaan Majid (5)
Cheadle Hulme Primary School, Cheadle

Play

P laying in the rain is fun
L ook at all the children playing in the rain
A h, I can't hear you because you are too far away from me
Y ay, I love playing with Mr Ince.

Jessica Healen (5)
Cheadle Hulme Primary School, Cheadle

Play

P eople playing in the playground and having fun on the swing
L earning in a classroom
A ctivities for the classroom
Y o-yos are fun to play with your friends.

Charlotte Grace Marsden (6)
Cheadle Hulme Primary School, Cheadle

Play

P eople are playing in the rain and wind
L ook at my friends playing on the monkey bars
A n animal is playing with all the school
Y ay, let's go and play!

Ellen Travis (6)
Cheadle Hulme Primary School, Cheadle

Play

P laying across the street with my friends
L ibby and Lucia are playing catch
A lexander is playing drawing
Y ou are playing underneath a rainbow.

Libby Manion (5)
Cheadle Hulme Primary School, Cheadle

Play

P laying is good for you and it is fun
L ollipops are fun to eat
A moon rock is fun to see
Y ou can see people playing just like me.

Zidane Yahya Naveed (6)
Cheadle Hulme Primary School, Cheadle

Play

P laying is good for you
L ook out of the window
A lix likes to splash in the puddles
Y ay, lots of crocodiles live in the swamp!

Raya Malik (5)
Cheadle Hulme Primary School, Cheadle

Play

P eople play outside
L et's play together, it's fun
A nd I play today with my friend
Y ou play with me if you want to.

Jessica Rose Payne (5)
Cheadle Hulme Primary School, Cheadle

Play

P laying with my sister in the park
L et's play on the swings
A t my house, I am playing Play-Doh
Y ou let me play it.

Mila-Rose Usher (5)
Cheadle Hulme Primary School, Cheadle

Play

P lay in a puddle together
L aughing at a funny joke
A lexander likes playing in puddles
Y ay! Playing with Alexander.

Isaac Paul (5)
Cheadle Hulme Primary School, Cheadle

Play

P eople are laughing
L izard is climbing up the tree
A ll the people have a yo-yo
Y o-yos are bouncing up and down.

Noah Waite (5)
Cheadle Hulme Primary School, Cheadle

Play

P eople like playing
L ook out of the window, look they are playing
A ll of the people I like
Y ay, let's play!

Ellie Marsden (5)
Cheadle Hulme Primary School, Cheadle

Play

P laying is fun for me
L ollipops are fun for me too
A nimals are eating the grass
Y aks are charging at a rabbit.

Theo Davison (5)
Cheadle Hulme Primary School, Cheadle

Play

P icnic in the sunny park
L earning lovely activities
A dventure in the sunny park
Y o-yos bobbing up and down.

Ella Boyd (6)
Cheadle Hulme Primary School, Cheadle

Play

P eople are playing
L ook at a bird in the sky
A lexander is going to Farlova
Y ay, let's play together.

Olivia Heritage (5)
Cheadle Hulme Primary School, Cheadle

Play

P icnic with my friend
L ooking for bugs
A corns falling off the tree
Y ou throwing stones in the river.

Beatrice Blake (6)
Cheadle Hulme Primary School, Cheadle

Play

P lay pushing my Bobo on the swing
L ove playing on swings
A pples fall from the trees
Y ellow sun.

Hugo Tatton (5)
Cheadle Hulme Primary School, Cheadle

Play

P laying with my sister in my bedroom
L et's go people
A pple picking
Y ay, I am on the slide!

Imaan Maya Sheikh (5)
Cheadle Hulme Primary School, Cheadle

Play

P eople playing at the park
L earning at the park
A nts crawling at the park
Y ay, let's play!

Imogen Walker (5)
Cheadle Hulme Primary School, Cheadle

Play

P eople on the street at the park
L et's play!
A pples on the tree
Y o-yos going up and down.

Aariya Knight (5)
Cheadle Hulme Primary School, Cheadle

Play

P eople like playing
L ook at me, it is fun
A nimals like to play
Y ou can play with everyone.

Sebastian O'Neill (5)
Cheadle Hulme Primary School, Cheadle

Play

P laying with trains
L icking a lolly on a hot day
A m going on an adventure
Y o-yos are fun.

James Bailey (5)
Cheadle Hulme Primary School, Cheadle

Play

P ushing my brother on the swing
L icking a lolly on a hot day
A dventure in the park
Y eah!

Charlie Francis Coombes (5)
Cheadle Hulme Primary School, Cheadle

Play

P lay in the snow
L ook out the window
A lexander is happy
Y ay, let's play together.

Elsa Harling Kington (5)
Cheadle Hulme Primary School, Cheadle

Play

P eople play in the garden
L ooking for bugs
A bunch of people
Y o-yos are a toy.

Georgia Andrew (5)
Cheadle Hulme Primary School, Cheadle

Play

P lay with me
L ooking for bugs
A lways be kind
Y es, you can play.

Saul David White (5)
Cheadle Hulme Primary School, Cheadle

Play

P eople in the sunny park
L ike to play
A swing
Y o-yos.

Camilla Eaton (5)
Cheadle Hulme Primary School, Cheadle

Play

P ark path
L earn with leaves
A ctivities
Y ay!

Henry Charles Fitzmaurice (5)
Cheadle Hulme Primary School, Cheadle

Unicorn

U nicorns are very kind
N o unicorn has been mean
I mportant as a meeting
C heerful as a cheerleader
O ften flying not so far
R ome is too far to fly to
N ow do you know about unicorns?

Asiya Husna Sageer (6)
Fig Tree Primary School, Hyson Green

Dragon

D irilis Ertugrul the warrior
R oaring to go on a mission
A s speedy as a bow and arrow
G lamorous like the shiny armour
O n a mission with his Alps
N othing can get in their way.

Abbas Saqib (6)
Fig Tree Primary School, Hyson Green

Panther

P urr like a loud lion
A s fast as a jet
N ever afraid
T errifying
H ungry as a panda
E nthusiastic hunting
R oyal like a king.

Yahya Salahudeen Khan (6)
Fig Tree Primary School, Hyson Green

Gorilla

G rumpy as a baby
O dd as a monkey
R apid
I mportant like money
L arge as a car
L ots of fluffy fur
A ngry as Hulk.

Abdussami Butt (7)
Fig Tree Primary School, Hyson Green

Lion

L ives in the jungle
I t's very fierce
O n a log like a frog
N aughty like a monkey.

Zaynab Chishti (6)
Fig Tree Primary School, Hyson Green

Kindness

F reddie Jack is my name
R eally caring is my game
E arning extra pocket money
D usting really helps my mummy
D addy helps me clean my hamster
I n his cage, he's really pampered
E xtra help around the house.

J ust makes my mummy so, so proud
A va is my sister's name
C uddling her is really fun
K indness, that's how it's done.

Freddie Jack G (5)
Gilbert Heathcote Nursery & Infant School, Whittington Moor

Kali-Rose's Animals

K ittens are cute
A nts are scary
L ions have big teeth
I guanas stick their tongues out

R hinos have big horns
O striches run fast
S nakes slither
E lephants are huge.

Kali-Rose B (5)
Gilbert Heathcote Nursery & Infant School, Whittington Moor

Phoebe

P igs are my favourite animals
H ot chocolate is my favourite drink
O liver plays schools with me
E verything in my room is pink
B eaches are my favourite place
E ngland is where I live.

Phoebe Launt (5)
Gilbert Heathcote Nursery & Infant School, Whittington Moor

My Name

A utumn

B arnett
A unicorn is my best pet
R un all the way home
N ew toys are best
E very girl is good
T oys are my favourite
T oast is my favourite food.

Autumn Belle Barnett (6)
Gilbert Heathcote Nursery & Infant School, Whittington Moor

Suhrit

S pace is my favourite topic
U niverse is big
H ottest star in our galaxy is the sun
R ockets go faster than aeroplanes
I like black holes
T elescopes are good for looking into space.

Suhrit Gudekota (6)
Gilbert Heathcote Nursery & Infant School, Whittington Moor

Me And Mummy

M e and Mummy
A lways play
L ate at night
A nd in the day
Y esterday we played blocks
A nd today we will paint rocks
H ome time at last, it's the end of a lovely day.

Malayah Jayne D W (6)
Gilbert Heathcote Nursery & Infant School, Whittington Moor

Courtney

C hips I like to eat
O pening presents
U nicorns I like
R unning with my friends
T alking to family
N anna I love
E llie's my best friend
Y elling loudly.

Courtney S (5)
Gilbert Heathcote Nursery & Infant School, Whittington Moor

Funfair

S illy children shout and scream
O n the spinning wheel fast
P opcorn is not my favourite
H ot food is my favourite
I n the ballpit I jump
E veryone is having a fun time.

Sophie R (5)
Gilbert Heathcote Nursery & Infant School, Whittington Moor

Callen

C allen Alec is my name
A nd I go to Gilbert's School
L earning is what I do
L aughing is cool too
E nd the day with coats and bags
N ow home for tea and chill.

Callen Alec W (5)
Gilbert Heathcote Nursery & Infant School, Whittington Moor

Holly

H is for helpful
O is for orange, my favourite fruit
L oving my family is what I do
L is for like, I like to ride my bike
Y is for you're the best teacher ever.

Holly W (5)
Gilbert Heathcote Nursery & Infant School, Whittington Moor

Life

E very day starts when the sun rises
L ive a life full of fun
L ove, laugh and enjoy yourself
I sn't learning such fun?
S ummer is my favourite time of the year.

Ellis R (5)
Gilbert Heathcote Nursery & Infant School, Whittington Moor

My Life

S chool is fun
I like playing
E very day I learn
N ow I'm getting older
N ow I'm getting bigger
A nimals are the best.

Sienna Mae Gayles (5)
Gilbert Heathcote Nursery & Infant School, Whittington Moor

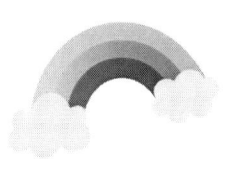

Khadija

K hadija
H er love is chicken
A rabbit loves carrots
D ig a road
I eat chips
J elly is yummy
A jelly is wobbly.

Khadija S (5)
Gilbert Heathcote Nursery & Infant School, Whittington Moor

Dolls Are Fun

M y dolls are fun
I like playing with them
L ike playing schools
L ots and lots
I love playing shops
E very day.

Millie Grace Houghton (6)
Gilbert Heathcote Nursery & Infant School, Whittington Moor

Ffion

F rosty morning walks
F ields full of friendly dogs
I love Mummy
O n towards home we go
N icely wrapped up with a hot cocoa.

Ffion Elizabeth L (6)
Gilbert Heathcote Nursery & Infant School, Whittington Moor

Keira

K eira saw the animals
E very weekend I dance
I like playing on the trampoline
R unning around
A cat is my pet.

Keira Elouise K (5)
Gilbert Heathcote Nursery & Infant School, Whittington Moor

About Eden

E lephants are my favourite animals
D rawing unicorns is fun
E very day I play on the monkey bars
N ever eat lemons.

Eden P (5)
Gilbert Heathcote Nursery & Infant School, Whittington Moor

Cory

C orythosaurus is a dino
O n holiday I like throwing stones in the ocean
R iding my bike
Y oghurts are my favourite.

Cory Max Shaw (5)
Gilbert Heathcote Nursery & Infant School, Whittington Moor

Lilly

L emons are too tangy
I ce cream is so yummy
L imes are so yucky
L ions have claws
Y o-yos are such fun.

Lilly hodgkiss (5)
Gilbert Heathcote Nursery & Infant School, Whittington Moor

Demi

D ancing is what I like to do
E veryone is pretty
M y best friend is Sienna
I love drawing pictures.

Demi Amber Taylor (5)
Gilbert Heathcote Nursery & Infant School, Whittington Moor

Kairi - All Around Us

K ites fly
A ll around us
I n the sky
R ound and high
I n the air, that one is mine.

Kairi Kiers D W (5)
Gilbert Heathcote Nursery & Infant School, Whittington Moor

William

W hite
I nsect
L ime
L emon
I gloo
A pple
M elon.

William Toft (6)
Gilbert Heathcote Nursery & Infant School, Whittington Moor

Faith

F antastic
A mazing
I ntelligent
T ruthful
H appy.

Faith C (5)
Gilbert Heathcote Nursery & Infant School, Whittington Moor

Dinosaurs

D inosaurs are scary
I like dinosaurs a little bit
N asty dinosaurs eat other dinos
O striches are better, badder than dinosaurs
S cience knows there were dinosaurs years ago
A dinosaur is scary
U nder the ground are dinosaur bones
R oar, roar, roar, the dinosaurs roar
S nakes slither on the ground.

Muhammad-Zayed Zaman (6)
Hannah Ball School, High Wycombe

Chocolate

C hocolate is my favourite snack
H as a lot of cream
O range cream inside
C reamy filling
O range and green cream
L ots of cream
A s big as a baby dragon
T eatime snack
E veryone loves chocolate.

Finley James Brittain (6)
Hannah Ball School, High Wycombe

Kitten

K ind wings help me to fly
I love to play with my pet
T he time I feed her makes her happy
T oo sparkly and shiny horn looks cute
E very day, I play with my kitten
N ice and shiny horn looks pretty on you.

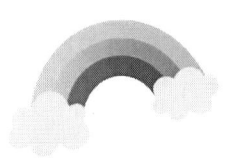

Aleema Afzal (6)
Hannah Ball School, High Wycombe

Friends

F reddie is a good friend
R eally fun time together
I like playing stuck in the mud
E mily is my sister
N icholas is my friend
D haram used to be my friend
S o have a good night.

Lily Miranda Rigby (7)
Hannah Ball School, High Wycombe

Unicorn

U seful glowing horn unicorn
N ice new sparkling horn
I have rainbow hair
C olourful stars when in the air
O n the unicorn horn are stars
R ed top hair
N ice looking hair.

Annetta Williams (6)
Hannah Ball School, High Wycombe

Cheetah

C heetahs are dangerous
H e has four legs
E at meat
E verything is afraid of cheetahs
T hey are very fast
A cheetah is fast
H e eats meat because he's a carnivore.

Owais Akhtar (6)
Hannah Ball School, High Wycombe

Rabbit

R abbits are so fluffy and wiggles its nose
A around the rabbit hutch it hops
B ouncy and fluffy
B ig and fluffy
I love rabbits
T ime to play.

Mia Grace Green (7)
Hannah Ball School, High Wycombe

Dragon

D ragons are dangerous
R oaring
A dragon likes to breathe fire
G ot big jaws
O h my god, that is a dragon
N ot everyone likes dragons.

Ayaan Abbas (6)
Hannah Ball School, High Wycombe

Beach

B oats in the sea
E veryone's got an ice cream
A ll people have fun
C rabs are done with the people
H ot day to play on the beach.

Kira Zielinska (6)
Hannah Ball School, High Wycombe

Fluffy

F luffy dog
L ikes to run
U nlikely friends
F un to play with my dog
F riendly dog
Y ay, my dog likes to sleep.

Freddie Bailey Stevens (6)
Hannah Ball School, High Wycombe

Puppy

P uppies are cute
U nlikely friends
P uppies are playing with the ball
P uppies are so good
Y ou are my friend.

Nicholas Paraskiv (6)
Hannah Ball School, High Wycombe

Beach

B uild a sandcastle
E veryone loves the beach
A whale moved
C hildren are playing
H ot day on the beach.

Antony Kupiec (6)
Hannah Ball School, High Wycombe

Fox

F ox is sleeping
O nto the light
X -rays are all about the fun.

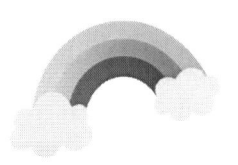

Brooke Ives (5)
Hannah Ball School, High Wycombe

Caleb Hamilton

C lumsy
A ugust is my birthday
L ollies are tasty
E very day I play with my friends
B ubbly.

H amilton is my second name
A nts are small
M y favourite drink is hot chocolate
I play with my friend
L ady Alice is my school
T hink
O ranges are good
N osy.

Caleb Hamilton (7)
Lady Alice Primary School, Greenock

Morgan Crossan

M y favourite kind of cat is grey
O rla is my friend
R ed is a nice colour
G reen is a colour
A nna is my bestie
N osy.

C lover is my cat
R unning is fun
O liver is a name
S ummer is my friend
S un is nice
A lways kind
N ice, my bed is cosy.

Morgan Vicki Crossan (6)
Lady Alice Primary School, Greenock

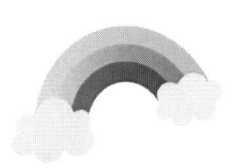

Alan Docherty

A pril is my birthday month
L ady Alice is the school I go to
A rt is my favourite subject
N osy.

D ad is funny
O ranges are tasty
C lothes are comfy
H appy
E ggs are bad
R ed is my favourite colour
T ennis is fun
Y oghurt is my favourite food.

Alan Docherty (7)
Lady Alice Primary School, Greenock

Orla Mcmillan

O rla is my name
R ed is my favourite colour
L ovely
A pples.

M y favourite story is Mister Nosey
C lumsy
M essy
I love my mum
L. O.L.s are nice toys
L orna is Abbie's mum
A leksandra is my friend
N osy.

Orla McMillan (6)
Lady Alice Primary School, Greenock

Aleksandra

A lways smiling
L ong hair
E ggs
K ind to my sister
S pecial
A wesome
N osy
D ark hair and eyes
R ainbows
A lways laughing.

Aleksandra Da Fonseca (6)
Lady Alice Primary School, Greenock

Summer

S ummer is my name
U nderwater swimming
M iss Campbell is my teacher
M edium is my size
E very day I try my best
R ed is my favourite colour.

Summer Williams Docherty (6)
Lady Alice Primary School, Greenock

Zak Arthur

Z oo
A nimal
K ick.

A rt
R oad
T rain
H ippo
U sually good
R espectful.

Zak Arthur (7)
Lady Alice Primary School, Greenock

Deryn

D aring Deryn
E xciting magic
R espectful
Y ellow
N ice.

Deryn Paul (6)
Lady Alice Primary School, Greenock

Kian

K ian is my name
I have a pet
A iden is my brother
N aps are good.

Kian Deehan-Cowan (7)
Lady Alice Primary School, Greenock

Noah-Hussain

N ever giving up
O ranges are yummy
A pples are my favourite
H appy, smiley Spider-Man face.

H eroic like my superheroes
U nique style
S uperstar
S weet as berry
A lways be myself
I lluminating star
N ever-ending shining light.

Noah-Hussain Mahmood-Gupta (5)
Normanhurst School, North Chingford

Toyosi Francesca

F ran loves vanilla ice cream
R unning is my favourite thing to do
A sweet would be nice
N ot many people know that I bake cakes
C hocolate is my favourite
E gg is my favourite food to eat
S end me a letter
C an we go to the park?
A grey cat is in the zoo!

Toyosi Francesca Fagbemiro (6)
Normanhurst School, North Chingford

Niquey Lowe

N ice hair bobbles
I am pretty and I love my mummy
Q ueen of reading and dancing
U nderstanding science
E xciting holiday
Y ou are my best friend.

L ollipops are yummy
O h, you're here
W ow, where were you?
E ating is fun.

Kehanique Lowe (6)
Normanhurst School, North Chingford

Francesco

F ireworks are cool
R eading gives me information
A pples are sweet for me
N ever without my cheeky smile
C hocolate is good to eat
E veryone is super kind to me
S ports are special to me
C hampions are the winners
O ctopuses are weird.

Francesco Chechile (7)
Normanhurst School, North Chingford

Eden Ryan

E nergetic running makes me hyper
D ancing queen
E ating chocolate is wonderful
N ever give up.

R eally love my mum
Y ou can be my friend
A mazing at doing the splits
N ever let me change.

Eden Ryan (6)
Normanhurst School, North Chingford

Alicia

A licia sunbathes on the beach
L ike strawberry ice cream
I have a dog because I love them
C an't ride the horse at the market
I can paint a horse and a rainbow
A cat is fun because they follow the lace.

Alicia Shakeel (6)
Normanhurst School, North Chingford

Lillie

L illie is the best person ever
I love Christmas because I get presents
L ola is my teddy
L ollies are delicious and I love Twisters
I love my toys and my sister, Maisie
E ating I love to do every day.

Lillie Durrant (6)
Normanhurst School, North Chingford

Erin

E xtremely good at science
R eading is my best hobby ever because I can never stop reading
I like exploring and I love the forest, picking up conkers
N ever go in the dark without an adult because you might get lost.

Erin Fernandes (6)
Normanhurst School, North Chingford

Farah

F arah is a very good child
A lollipop is my favourite sweet
R ainbows are so colourful and only appear once in a while
A pricots are so juicy and bright yellow
H ome time is the best part of the day.

Farah Escoffery (6)
Normanhurst School, North Chingford

Zakariya

Z oo trip with my family
A lways having fun
K arate is super
A mazing and always good
R acing cars are fast
I never give up
Y ummy, crunchy crisps
A kind boy!

Zakariya Kodabuckus (5)
Normanhurst School, North Chingford

Korai

K orai likes to play with his toys every day
O r I would like to play with my rabbits
R unning is my favourite thing to do
A nd I like to go to Jump City
I want to go to the park.

Korai Masters (6)
Normanhurst School, North Chingford

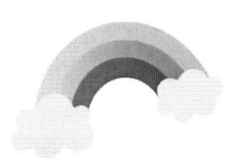

Emily

E very day I love Mummy
M um and Dad love each other
I am kind
L oving books about fairy tales
Y ummy, crunchy snacks.

Emily Freedlander (5)
Normanhurst School, North Chingford

James

J is for jam that's tasty
A mazing and impressive
M y name is James
E nergetic and fast
S wimming I like best.

James Rapacki-Gladwell (5)
Normanhurst School, North Chingford

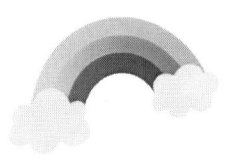

Kelly

K ittens are fluffy
E ggs are tasty
L ovely and caring
L ove Barbie dolls
Y ellow ducks swimming.

Kelly Ana Tranchand (5)
Normanhurst School, North Chingford

Irina

I love school
R eally good at writing
I love Aladdin
N ice to my friends
A mazing at reading.

Irina Khairutdinova (5)
Normanhurst School, North Chingford

Nina

N ina likes to swim
I like to do gymnastics
N ina likes to do ballet
A nd I like to lick ice cream.

Nina Evans (6)
Normanhurst School, North Chingford

Izah

I like school because it is fun
Z oo trips with my mum
A mazing with my work
H orses galloping.

Izah Mirza (5)
Normanhurst School, North Chingford

Emran

E nergetic
M ultisports are fun
R is for running
A mazing and fast
N ot rude.

Emran Qazi-Hoq (5)
Normanhurst School, North Chingford

Enis

E nergetic at running
N ever rude
I love dinosaurs
S tories are my favourite.

Enis Hacimusa (6)
Normanhurst School, North Chingford

Cats

C ute cats
A mazingly sweet
T ired sometimes
S leepy, lazy cats.

Caitlin McGuinness (6)
Normanhurst School, North Chingford

Unicorn Dream

U nicorns are my favourite things
N ever have I stroked one
I think they are beautiful
C olourful and magical
O ver the rainbow far away
R unning and sometimes flying
N ever seen a unicorn
S ometimes they come to me in my dreams.

Ruby Hannaford (6)
Roughwood Primary School, Rotherham

Unicorn

U nicorns have rainbow tails
N ice to look at with their glitter and sparkles
I think they are magical
C olours are bright
O n their heads they have an ice cream cone
R eally beautiful with their different colours
N ever get bored of them.

Layla Rose Evans (6)
Roughwood Primary School, Rotherham

My Amazing Family

F amily is very important to me
A lways love and respect each other
M ummy and Daddy are very special to me
I love my family a lot
L ove your family forever and ever
Y ou can give your family hugs and kisses.

Holly Garrity (6)
Roughwood Primary School, Rotherham

Sophia Taylor

S hooting at the goal is important
O ur country is Scotland
P eople in my family love me
H appier is my favourite song
I like chocolate and wraps
A n iPod is all I want!

T an is what I like to get in the summer
A big chocolate bar is the best
Y oghurt is the worst
L ollipops are good
O n my trampoline I do backflips
R are toys I like!

Sophia Taylor (7)
St Peter's Primary School, Paisley

Joe Hannigan

J avelin I would like to do
O rla is my sister
E very trophy I would like to gain.

H annigan is my last name
A ndrew is my best friend
N othing to me is ever the end
N umber eight is my favourite
I really like to go for a slumber
G race is my mum's name
A nimals I would like to get
N ever will I go on a jet.

Joe Hannigan (8)
St Peter's Primary School, Paisley

Orla Hannigan

O rla is my name
R iding horses I love to do
L ove unicorns so much!
A packet of crisps is my favourite snack.

H olographic images I love
A guinea pig I would love to have
N ight-time I hate!
N ever stop practising piano
I love dancing
G oing for a run too
A nightmare is horrible
N ever give up!

Orla Hannigan (8)
St Peter's Primary School, Paisley

Joanna Shibu

J oanna Shibu is my name
O ur class is a fantastic place
A fairy is my favourite toy
N ever stop learning
N early no rest
A fun game in the sun.

S hoes that are red I love
H orses are very lovely
I also love unicorns
B usy me, I am so crazy
U nder the bright sun I lie.

Joanna Shibu (8)
St Peter's Primary School, Paisley

Amazing Aiden

A lot of teddies
M y iPad is fun
A mazing at art
Z apping through games
I like Pokémon
N inja weapons
G reninja is my favourite.

A rt for kids hub is the best
I like marshmallows
D eath is my fear
E lectronics are the best
N ever enough sweets.

Aiden Mark McCafferty (7)
St Peter's Primary School, Paisley

Leah Rules

L ove unicorns, they are my favourite animal
E lectronics are the best
A pple is my favourite snack
H oney is the best!

R eading is my favourite subject
U nderneath the lights I toil
L ove animals so much
E va is my best friend
S pelling is great fun!

Leah Jackson (7)
St Peter's Primary School, Paisley

Brandon

B randon is my name
R ugby is a tough game
A llison is my second name
N o days off football
D inosaurs are interesting to me
O n Christmas Day, hopefully I get presents
N ever stop practising football.

Brandon Allison (7)
St Peter's Primary School, Paisley

Mialena

M ialena is my name
I love being in this school
A cold popsicle under the hot sun
L ightning is scary
E llie is my best friend
N ever stop learning
A unicorn is my favourite animal.

Mialena Craig (8)
St Peter's Primary School, Paisley

Andrew

A ndrew is my name
N ever stop playing football
D are a lot, like a devil
R eally hate dancing!
E than is my friend
W ant to be the best footballer in the world!

Andrew Herd (8)
St Peter's Primary School, Paisley

Ethan

E pic boy
T eaching football is my favourite thing
H aving goals in my garden would be great
A tiger is my favourite animal
N othing can stop me playing amazingly well!

Ethan Kennedy (8)
St Peter's Primary School, Paisley

Ciaran

C urly fries I hate
I am athletic
A lion is my favourite animal
R oaring like I sometimes do
A brilliant love is computers
N ew teachers are the best.

Ciaran McCall (8)
St Peter's Primary School, Paisley

School

S it in your seat all day
C old days, indoor play
H appy break times
O ur school is the best
O ur library is for reading
L oving this important place.

Ellie Fadian (8)
St Peter's Primary School, Paisley

Niamh

N iamh is my name
I like to go shopping
A pples are my favourite fruit
M y dog is cute
H i, I like sweets.

Niamh Banaghan (7)
St Peter's Primary School, Paisley

Max

M y favourite food is an apple
A Fortnite play is an important time
X box is the worst!

Max William Crawford (8)
St Peter's Primary School, Paisley

My Pets

M y dog is called Teddy
Y apping is what he does when I leave.

P ip and Boo are my fish
E ating is what they like to do the most
T hey are goldfish but one's black and the other's orange
S ome day I would like a pet dog called Doug the Pug.

Olivia Highway (6)
St Thomas Of Canterbury Catholic Primary School, Coalpool

Donald

D earest, my life thine
O ptimistic always and open-minded to new ideas
N ever give up when you are after what you seek
A lways remember you are beautiful and unique
L et me be creative
D emonstrate knowledge to show the world what I can do.

Donald Munachimso Nwonyi (7)
St Thomas Of Canterbury Catholic Primary School, Coalpool

Ireland

I have travelled there by ferry
R elatives of mine live there
E veryone is so nice
L ots of Ireland is luscious
A nd green
N ever have I ever been somewhere so beautiful
D ublin is the best capital city in the world.

Saoirse Beau Larmour (6)
St Thomas Of Canterbury Catholic Primary School, Coalpool

Rainbow

R ed is one of my colours
A lways beautiful
I n the sky is where I live
N ext to me is maybe a pot of gold
B eware, I'm not here for long
O ver the hill is where you will see me
W ind, rain and sun form me.

Nelly Baumgardt (5)
St Thomas Of Canterbury Catholic Primary School, Coalpool

My Biggest Wish

U nicorn, Unicorn, let me touch your horn
N obody knows where you were born
I always asked my mom
C an I have one?
O ne day she said okay
R ed and white and magical
N ever had a better one.

Hanna Skulska (6)
St Thomas Of Canterbury Catholic Primary School, Coalpool

Orla Rae

O rla Rae is my name
R ed is my favourite colour
L ove my family lots
A tiger is my favourite animal.

R eading books is so much fun
A wesome big sister
E verybody loves my smile.

Orla Rae Larmour (5)
St Thomas Of Canterbury Catholic Primary School, Coalpool

Favourite Player

R uns like a car
O verpowers the goalkeeper
N ice house in Madrid
A wesome player
L ikes to train
D angerous opponent
O riginal football style.

Benjamin Tryjankowski (6)
St Thomas Of Canterbury Catholic Primary School, Coalpool

Marley

M akes me smile
A lways plays with me
R uns a lot
L ove him so much
E ats a lot
Y es he is my best friend.

Oliwier Donaj (6)
St Thomas Of Canterbury Catholic Primary School, Coalpool

Write

W ild animals are scary
R abbits are not
I will never touch a lion
T iger and a snake
E lephants do not moan.

Skyla Kenfack (6)
St Thomas Of Canterbury Catholic Primary School, Coalpool

Young Writers Information

We hope you have enjoyed reading this book – and that you will continue to in the coming years.

If you're a young writer who enjoys reading and creative writing, or the parent of an enthusiastic poet or story writer, do visit our website www.youngwriters.co.uk. Here you will find free competitions, workshops and games, as well as recommended reads, a poetry glossary and our blog. There's lots to keep budding writers motivated to write!

If you would like to order further copies of this book, or any of our other titles, then please give us a call or order via your online account.

Young Writers
Remus House
Coltsfoot Drive
Peterborough
PE2 9BF
(01733) 890066
info@youngwriters.co.uk

Join in the conversation!
Tips, news, giveaways and much more!

YoungWritersUK   @YoungWritersCW